Brilliant Activities for

Grammar and Punctuation, Year 1

Activities for Developing and Reinforcing Key Language Skills

Irene Yates

Brilliant
PUBLICATIONS

This set of books is dedicated to the memory of Miss Hannah Gamage and to the children of St. Philip Neri with St. Bede's Catholic Primary School, Mansfield.

• •

We hope you and your pupils enjoy using the ideas in this book. Brilliant Publications publishes many other books to help primary school teachers. To find out more details on all of our titles, including those listed below, please log onto our website: www.brilliantpublications.co.uk.

Other books in the **Brilliant Activities for Grammar and Punctuation Series**

	Printed ISBN	e-pdf ISBN
Year 2	978-1-78317-126-2	978-1-78317-133-0
Year 3	978-1-78317-127-9	978-1-78317-134-7
Year 4	978-1-78317-128-6	978-1-78317-135-4
Year 5	978-1-78317-129-3	978-1-78317-136-1
Year 6	978-1-78317-130-9	978-1-78317-137-8

Brilliant Activities for Creative Writing Series

Year 1	978-0-85747-463-6
Year 2	978-0-85747-464-3
Year 3	978-0-85747-465-0
Year 4	978-0-85747-466-7
Year 5	978-0-85747-467-4
Year 6	978-0-85747-468-1

Brilliant Activities for Reading Comprehension Series

Year 1	978-1-78317-070-8
Year 2	978-1-78317-071-5
Year 3	978-1-78317-072-2
Year 4	978-1-78317-073-9
Year 5	978-1-78317-074-6
Year 6	978-1-78317-075-3

Published by Brilliant Publications
Unit 10
Sparrow Hall Farm
Edlesborough
Dunstable
Bedfordshire
LU6 2ES, UK

Email: info@brilliantpublications.co.uk
Website: www.brilliantpublications.co.uk
Tel: 01525 222292

The name Brilliant Publications and the logo are registered trademarks.

Written by Irene Yates
Illustrated by Molly Sage
Front cover illustration by Brilliant Publications

© Text Irene Yates 2015
© Design Brilliant Publications 2015
Printed ISBN 978-1-78317-125-5
e-pdf ISBN 978-1-78317-132-3

First printed and published in the UK in 2015

The right of Irene Yates to be identified as the author of this work has been asserted by herself in accordance with the Copyright, Designs and Patents Act 1988.

Learn the alphabet 2

Hello, I'm Punc. Today, Gram and I are here to help you learn the ALPHABET. The alphabet is made up of letters. Here are some letters:
U V W x y z

There are two kinds of letters – big ones and small ones.

BIG letters are called **CAPITAL** letters.

Small letters are called **lower case** letters.

Copy these small letters and say their *sounds* in this order.

a   b   c   d   e   f   g   h   i

----

j   k   l   m   n   o   p   q

----

r   s   t   u   v   w   x   y   z

> **Look for CAPITAL letters and small letters in a storybook together.**

Avoid adding the 'uh' sound to letter sounds.

Alphabetical order

When you know the alphabet, you know that all the letters come in a special order.

This is called **alphabetical order**.

We use it all the time because it makes things easy for us.

Henry   Izzy   Adam   Daisy   Mani

If the children lined up in alphabetical order, they would be:

Adam Daisy Henry Izzy Mani

Get into groups of six and arrange yourselves into alphabetical order. Write your names in alphabetical order here:

1. _____   4. _____

2. _____   5. _____

3. _____   6. _____

Talk about the letters in your names and what order they come in the alphabet.

If the children found this easy, try with the whole class; help them arrange themslves into alphabetical order.

Brilliant Activities for Grammar and Punctuation, Year 1
© Irene Yates and Brilliant Publications

How much do you know?

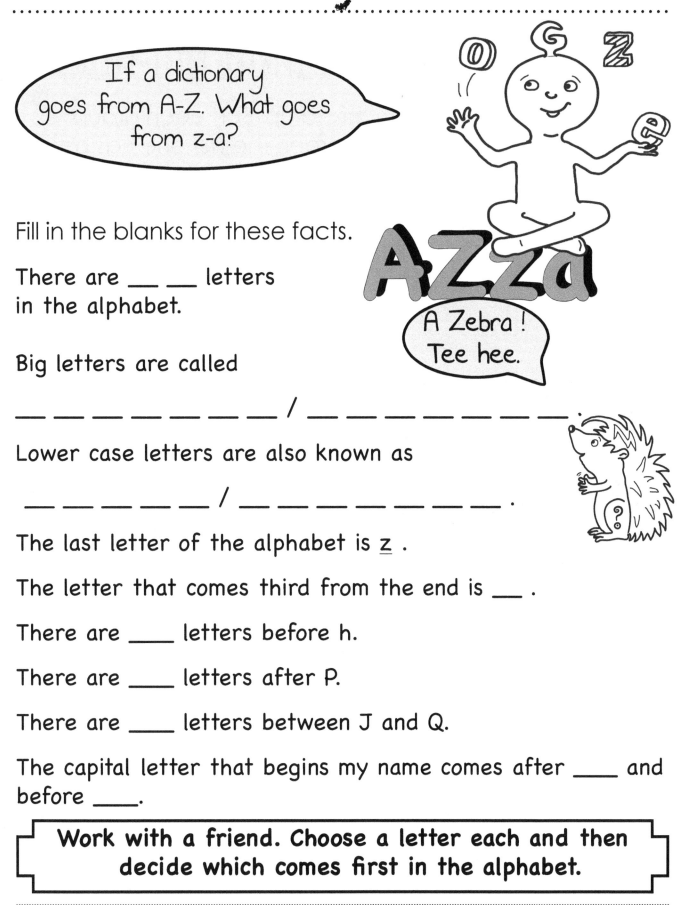

If a dictionary goes from A-Z. What goes from z-a?

A Zebra! Tee hee.

Fill in the blanks for these facts.

There are __ __ letters in the alphabet.

Big letters are called

__ __ __ __ __ __ __ / __ __ __ __ __ __ __ __ .

Lower case letters are also known as

__ __ __ __ __ / __ __ __ __ __ __ __ __ .

The last letter of the alphabet is <u>z</u> .

The letter that comes third from the end is __ .

There are ____ letters before h.

There are ____ letters after P.

There are ____ letters between J and Q.

The capital letter that begins my name comes after ____ and before ____.

Work with a friend. Choose a letter each and then decide which comes first in the alphabet.

Involve the children in creating more alphabet facts.

Jumbled Letters

a	b	c	d	e	f	g	h	i	j	k	l	m	n	o	p	q	r	s	t	u	v	w	x	y	z

All these letters have been mixed up. Sort each group into the correct alphabetical order. The first one has been done for you.

BAC = ABC

FHG = _____

DBEC = _____

RSPQ = _____

gfe = _____

vut = _____

rqop = _____

yzxw = _____

monl = _____

Jumble-up some letters and get your friend to put them into alphabetical order.

_____   _____

_____   _____

Call out a letter to your friend who then has to say the three letters that come before or after it.

Repeat as often as necessary until children understand the concept of alphabetical order.

Brilliant Activities for Grammar and Punctuation, Year 1
© Irene Yates and Brilliant Publications

Alphabet poem

Here is a poem that will help you to remember the alphabet. The poem is not finished. Turn this sheet over and finish it by yourself, with another person, or in your group.

A is for animal, able and all

B is for biscuit, batting and ball

C is for calendar, candle and corn

D is for dancing and dewdrop and dawn

E is for everything, elbow and eat

F is for funny and froggy and feet

G is for giggle and grandad and ghost

H is for happy and hero and host.

I is for island and illness and iffy

J is for jungle and jelly and jiffy

K is for kingdom and knick-knack and knot

L is for library and learning and lot

Stress rhythm and rhyme. Gather lots of rhyming words and make notes for the children to work from.

Is it a sentence?

A sentence is a group of words that makes sense on its own. Read the words and tick ✓ the boxes:

> **Warning**
> Just because a group of words starts with a capital letter and ends with a full stop, exclamation mark or question mark, it doesn't mean it's a sentence.

	This is a sentence	This isn't a sentence
1. As the dog.		
2. On the bus.		
3. The sun shone.		
4. Arrived.		
5. The bus was late.		
6. Everyone watched.		
7. And the bus driver.		
8. Jumped on.		
9. Scratched his head in amazement.		

Can you put these groups of words together to make a story written in proper sentences?

_ _

_ _

_ _

_ _

_ _

Take turns to say something silly to your friend. Together decide if it's a sentence or not.

Talk about how sentences make sense on their own. Let the children practise forming sentences orally before they try to write them down.

Brilliant Activities for Grammar and Punctuation, Year 1
© Irene Yates and Brilliant Publications

Collecting sentences

Choose a book from your book shelf. Flip through the pages. Choose six short sentences from the book and copy them here.

_ _ _ _ _ _ _ _ _ _ _ _ _ _ _ _ _ _ _ _

_ _ _ _ _ _ _ _ _ _ _ _ _ _ _ _ _ _ _ _

_ _ _ _ _ _ _ _ _ _ _ _ _ _ _ _ _ _ _ _

_ _ _ _ _ _ _ _ _ _ _ _ _ _ _ _ _ _ _ _

_ _ _ _ _ _ _ _ _ _ _ _ _ _ _ _ _ _ _ _

What is your book called? _ _ _ _ _ _ _ _ _ _ _

Who is the author? _ _ _ _ _ _ _ _ _ _ _ _ _ _

How much, out of 10, do you like it? _ _ _ _ _ _ _ _

With a friend, look for sentences in a book or comic. Cut, paste and stick them on a sheet of paper.

Help the children to recognise where a sentence begins and ends. Explain that we use punctuation to help make writing easier to understand.

Full stops or ... ?

> Sometimes a sentence doesn't have a full stop at the end. It might have an exclamation mark (!) or a question mark (?) instead.

A sentence that tells you something ends with a **full stop** .

> It is hot. The sun is shining today. I am rowing my boat.

A sentence that asks you something has a **question mark ?**

> Can you row a boat? Do you want a go?

A sentence that expresses strong feelings has an **exclamation mark !** at the end.

> Watch out! I won! What a great day!

Write one sentence of your own for each type. Remember: all sentences begin with a capital letter.

_ _

_ _

_ _

Challenge each other to say sentences that would end with a full stop (.), a question mark (?) and an exclamation mark (!).

Help the children to formulate their own sentences and share with the class verbally. Write up all the sentences and display them.

Brilliant Activities for Grammar and Punctuation, Year 1
© Irene Yates and Brilliant Publications

Making sentences

Sentences have a part that tells you who or what did something and what they did.

Draw lines to match the beginnings with the endings:

The girl	quacked.
The dog	left a trail.
A duck	has humps.
Dad	barked at the cat.
Robins	baked a cake.
A camel	can fly.
The snail	went swimming.

Write three new sentences. Remember: a sentence needs to make sense.

_ _

_ _

_ _

Challenge a friend to give the beginning of a sentence. Make up a funny ending. Take turns.

Talk through the examples with the children. With small group input, make up ten more as a puzzle to present to the class.

Add an ending

Choose the best word to complete each sentence.

I can climb

A sentence must make sense and must contain a verb - a doing or being word.

_____ .

(a street   this mountain   a hat)

We wear boots _____

(for dancing   for climbing   to skip)

Mountains are _____ .

(flat   grassy   high)

A clock tell us _____ .

(the weather   a phone call   the time)

Add endings of your own to complete these sentences:

A friend can _____ .

A giant is _____ .

Fish can _____ .

A door can _____ .

Tell each other all the things you can do.

Have lots of talking and oral work. After checking, give verbal beginnings of sentences for children to end. Also ask for endings from children for others to supply beginnings.

Brilliant Activities for Grammar and Punctuation, Year 1
© Irene Yates and Brilliant Publications

And, and, and ...

Sometimes you can join sentences together by using the word 'and'.

Remember: 'and' is a joining word.

Join these sentences together using 'and'.
Write the new sentence underneath.

1. I went to the park.   I played ball with a friend.

_____

2. I saw a girl on a skateboard.   She fell off.

_____

3. I went to the cafe.   I bought a bottle of water.

_____

4. There were lots of geese.   They chased me.

_____

5. It started to rain.   I went home.

_____

Start with a sentence. A friend adds 'and' and another sentence, then you add 'and' and another sentence. See how many sentences you can add.

Do the sticky tape trick. Tear a piece of paper in half, join it together with the tape. Write two short sentences on the whiteboard and demonstrate how the word 'and' acts like a piece of tape, joining the sentences together.

Brilliant Activities for Grammar and Punctuation, Year 1
© Irene Yates and Brilliant Publications

This page may be photocopied for use by the purchasing institution only.

17

More about 'and'

Remember 'and' can join two sentences together.

TIP: when you join two sentences together with 'and' the second one does not keep its capitol letter.

Finish off these sentences in your own way. Remember, your half has to be a sentence as well. Think carefully!

1. I went to the shop **and** I _____

2. My friends came round **and** we _____

3. An elephant is massive **and** it _____

4. Fish can swim **and** birds _____

5. I like ice cream **and** I _____

6. I can jump **and** I _____

7. The dog barked **and** that _____

8. I play the drums **and** my _____

Take turns to start and finish sentences by joining two sentences. Make them funny.

Practise joining two sentences together with 'and' verbally. Share sentences aloud when all have finished.

Brilliant Activities for Grammar and Punctuation, Year 1
© Irene Yates and Brilliant Publications

Nouns are names

Nouns are the names of things around us. If things didn't have names we would get in a muddle.

Hey You, can you bring me that thing from the thing, please?

Fill in the blanks to give names to these things.

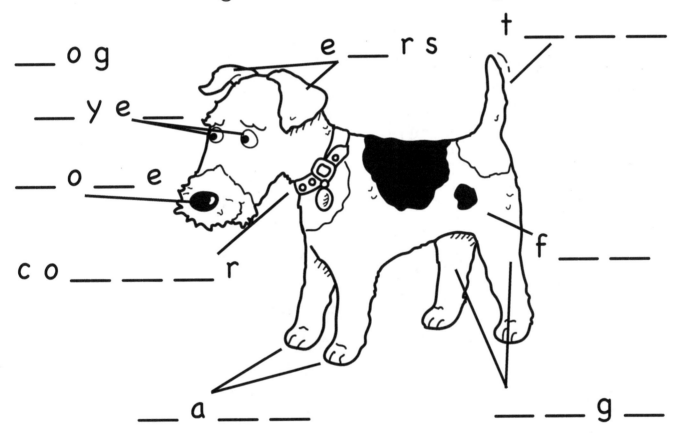

__ o g

e __ r s

t __ __ __ __

__ y e __

__ o __ e

c o __ __ __ __ r

f __ __ __

__ a __ __ __

__ __ __ g __

Tell your friend some of the things YOU have. Listen to some of the things your friend has.

Make sure all the children know the words for the different parts of the dog's body before they look at the diagram.

What can you see?

Write down the nouns of the things you can see in the pictures.

_____

_____

_____

_____

_____

_____

_____

_____

_____

_____

How many 'things' can you both think of in five minutes?

Talk through the picture with the children's input before they do the sheet. Share verbally when all have finished.

Brilliant Activities for Grammar and Punctuation, Year 1
© Irene Yates and Brilliant Publications

Noun puzzle

You know that nouns are the names of things. Solve these puzzles:

1. I have big ears.
   I have four feet.
   I have a trunk
   I am an _____.

2. I am high in the sky.
   I am a long way away.
   I twinkle in the dark.
   I am a _____.

3. I have a shell.
   I am laid by birds.
   I might hatch.
   I am an _____.

4. You can push me.
   I have wheels.
   Babies sit in me.
   I am a _____.

5. I have doors.
   I have a boot.
   You can drive me.
   I am a _____.

6. I climb and leap.
   I hang on trees.
   I am furry.
   I am a _____.

Now make up two noun puzzles of your own.

_____   _____

_____   _____

_____   _____

_____   _____

How many animals can you think of in five minutes?

Make up two or three puzzles on the board, with pupil input, to demonstrate how to do this puzzle.

Noun word puzzle

Look at the pictures. Find the name of each thing in the wordsearch puzzle. Write its name on the line below it.

_____ _____ _____

_____ _____ _____

b	o	o	k	s	b
f	r	o	g	i	a
d	u	c	k	n	b
n	s	e	o	g	y
m	o	o	n	w	z

Can you find an extra word in the puzzle?

_____

Make up a noun wordsearch puzzle together.

Ensure the children know what the pictures are before they look for the words in the wordsearch grid.

Brilliant Activities for Grammar and Punctuation, Year 1
© Irene Yates and Brilliant Publications

One or more than one?

Nouns can be **singular** (one) or **plural** (more than one). For most nouns we can just add an 's' to make them plural.

Try these.

| one cat | → two _____ | one dinosaur | → two _____ |

| one boat | → two _____ | one tree | → three _____ |

| one horse | → three _____ | one boy | → three _____ |

| one elephant | → four _____ | one girl | → four _____ |

How do you make SEVEN even?

Remove the **S**! Tee hee.

Make up some of your own.

| one _____ | → ___ _____ | one _____ | → ___ _____ |

Get the children used to using the words singular and plural. Reiterate frequently what they mean. Look for singular and plural nouns in storybooks and display a collection.

Different endings

We know that a singular noun is **one**.

You know that a plural noun is **more than one**.

We know that to make most singular nouns plural, you add an **S**: girls.

Words that already end in **s** or **x** or **ch** are different. We have to add 'es' instead of just 's'. Complete this table:

one	more than one
bus	buses
glass	glasses
dress	
kiss	
class	
fox	
box	
witch	
pitch	
church	

Think up nouns that end with 'S' together. Make them plural and listen to the end sound.

Get the children to suggest more singular nouns ending in s, ch or x.

Brilliant Activities for Grammar and Punctuation, Year 1
© Irene Yates and Brilliant Publications

Make a long, long, long sentence story

We've all heard the story about the house that Jack built.

It starts with a sentence that gets longer and longer. We can make up a story like that. The first sentence is:

This is the park where Jake plays.
This is the street that has the park where Jake plays.
This is the gate that's in the street that has the park where Jake plays.

How many more parts can you add?

Write some ideas here and share them. See how long you can make your sentence story.

_____

_____

_____

_____

Together see how much of the 'The House that Jack Built' you can say aloud.

Read 'The House that Jack Built' to the children. Point out how the story gets longer and longer but remains as one sentence. Show the text. Display class story with artwork.

Make a sentence

Cut out these boxes and fit them together to make proper sentences. Make sure they make sense!

✂ ------------------------------------

I	likes the weekend.
My friend	have whiskers.
Our dog	makes us laugh.
My teacher	want to play.
We are	likes ice cream.
Birds	love playing football.
Cats	going on a trip.
My dad	we always have circle time.
On Mondays	have feathers.
The boys	barks at people.

In pairs, one of you puts down the beginning of the sentence and your partner finishes it.

Cut and stick. Make sure the children understand the words must be right together, ie they can't have 'I likes ice-cream'. You can go through the phrases verbally to make nonsense sentences before they stick the boxes down.

Brilliant Activities for Grammar and Punctuation, Year 1
© Irene Yates and Brilliant Publications

Joining sentences

We know that we can join sentences together with the word 'and'. Make each set of sentences into one sentence, like this:

Dogs can run.   **Dogs can wag their tails.**
Dogs can run and they can wag their tails.

Bees buzz.   Bees collect pollen.

and
_____

Birds have feathers.   Birds build nests.

and
_____

Snakes are long.   Snakes lay eggs.

and
_____

Elephants are huge.   Elephants have tusks.

and
_____

Cats have fur.   Cats meow.

and
_____

Lions are big cats.   Lions roar.

and
_____

Rabbits have big ears.   Rabbits twitch their noses.

and
_____

Take turns to start. Say a short sentence then add 'and'. Allow your partner to complete it.

Go through all the sentences verbally first. Make sure all children can 'read' them. Help with scribing.

Let's describe

Adjectives are describing words. They tell us what something (a noun) is like. Think of some adjectives for these nouns.

| a _____ bug | a _____ pet |
| a _____ game | a _____ friend |

Draw one of the four nouns. Write a sentence underneath your picture to describe it.

How many adjectives can you think of to describe your school?

Ask for verbal suggestions for adjectives to go with each noun before the children complete this task. Have lots of discussion to ensure understanding of concept.

Brilliant Activities for Grammar and Punctuation, Year 1
© Irene Yates and Brilliant Publications

Which are?

Adjectives are describing words. We can put an adjective and a noun together, like this:

noun		adjective		
dog	+	playful	=	a playful dog
day	+	sunny	=	a sunny day
tree	+	shady	=	_____
story	+	good	=	_____
bird	+	yellow	=	_____
frog	+	green	=	_____
girl	+	happy	=	_____
boy	+	laughing	=	_____

Underline the adjectives:

The grass is green.

The ducklings are yellow.

The sky is blue.

The kitten has soft fur.

The circle is round.

The boy has strong hands.

REMEMBER: Nouns are naming words. Adjectives are describing words.

Work in pairs, one gives a noun, the other adds an adjective. Swap.

Use lots of talking to introduce this task. Read the words and sentences aloud. Ask the children to suggest nouns/ adjectives. Ask for more examples, eg what else could be green? How else might a bird be described?

Cut and stick

Here are some nouns and some adjectives. Cut them out and stick them down so that they go together.

mouse	long
ice lolly	sharp
car	soft
tail	cold
knife	small
water	dry
door	deep
pillow	open
banana	cheeky
washing	fast
monkey	ripe

Make up more nouns and adjectives to cut and stick.

Go through concepts of nouns and adjectives again. Help with reading, especially after the words are cut and being paired. Read again and share once paired.

Brilliant Activities for Grammar and Punctuation, Year 1
© Irene Yates and Brilliant Publications

What do you think?

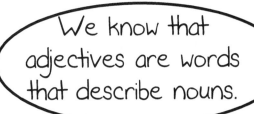 We know that adjectives are words that describe nouns.

What do you think these words might be describing?

foggy	1.		rainy
sunny			hot

round	2.		sticky
sweet			creamy

funny	3.		exciting
boring			picture

snug	4.		lace-up
flat			flip-flop

small	5.		croaking
green			leaping

fluffy	6.		cuddly
grey			lop-eared

Make up four adjectives to describe a cat, a friend and a forest.

Think of a noun. Desribe it to a friend using adjectives. Can they guess what it is? Swap roles.

If necessary, help with reading and scribing. Discuss all possibilities – the more talk, the better.

What's a verb?

Verbs are words that tell you what something or someone is doing.

We all do lots of things.

We:
sit   stand   walk   run
eat   jump   play   laugh

Can you think of eight more things we do? Fill in the missing letters to complete the doing words.

I can ___op.

I can ___ump.

I can ___ance.

I can ___it.

I can ___un.

I can ___ee.

I can ___alk.

I can ___ix.

TIP: go through the alphabet to find the missing letters.

Talk with a friend. Think of 25 things each of you can do.

Have lots of talk about doing or action words. Get the children to come out and perform an action for the group to guess.

Brilliant Activities for Grammar and Punctuation, Year 1

Changing the words

We can change our doing words or verbs by adding **'ing'** to the end of the word.

When I sleep I am <u>sleeping</u>.

When I eat I am _____ .

When I jump I am _____ .

When I fall I am _____ .

When I sail I am _____ .

When I talk I am _____ .

When I read I am _____ .

When I drink I am _____ .

When I _____ I am working.

When I _____ I am fishing.

When I _____ I am flying.

"ing" is called a suffix.

Work in pairs. Mime some actions. Get your partner to guess what you are doing. Swap.

Explain that sometimes we add endings to change a word. Talk through the task before beginning it.

Verbs and nouns together

Nouns are the names of things around us. Verbs are doing words. Let's put some nouns and verbs together.

Find some nouns and write the sentences.

What ticks? A clock ticks.

What quacks? _____

What barks? _____

What purrs? _____

What flies? _____

What shines? _____

What sails? _____

What swims? _____

Can you finish these sentences? (Tip: use a verb ending with the suffix 'ing'.)

The fish is _____

The clock is _____

The boat is _____

One calls out a verb and the other decides on the noun that does it. Swap.

Talk through the words on the page and the ideas before completing the task. Help with reading and scribing.

Brilliant Activities for Grammar and Punctuation, Year 1
© Irene Yates and Brilliant Publications

Make a proper sentence

We know that verbs are 'action' or 'doing' words.

We also know that a sentence is only a proper sentence when it has a verb in it.

Add a verb to each group of words to make proper sentences. The first one is done to show you how.

The teacher the story

The teacher **told** the story.

1. The girl _____ the ball.

2. The bell _____ for break.

3. Dad _____ an orange.

4. Jack _____ a banana.

5. Mum _____ in the sea.

6. Izzy _____ to the music.

7. A man _____ the door.

danced

paddled

closed

rang

bounced

peeled

ate

Read the sentences. Find the answers. Make the sentences silly by putting in the wrong verbs.

Go through each sentence carefully with children tracking the words. Look at the words. Verbalise sentences before writing. Some verbs can go in more than one sentence.

Proper nouns

We know that all things have names (nouns).

Some things also have proper names or 'proper nouns'.

Complete this puzzle. Don't forget to start your answers with a capital letter.

Proper nouns always begin with a capital letter.

a town _____

a boy's name _____

a day _____

a month _____

a country _____

a girl's name _____

Where do pencils go on holiday?

Pencil-vania! Tee, hee.

How many towns and countries can you think of together in 5 minutes?

Reinforce the concept of special names for people, places, days of the week, months, etc. Children should discuss this idea and give lots of examples before completing the task.

Days of the week

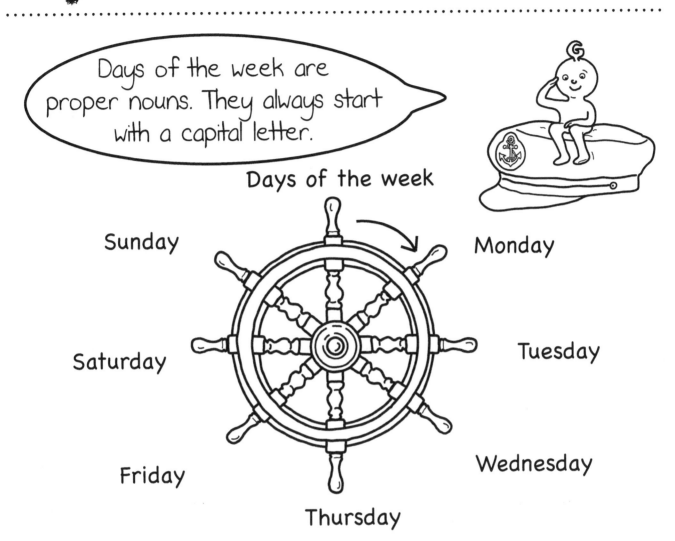

Days of the week are proper nouns. They always start with a capital letter.

Days of the week

Sunday

Monday

Saturday

Tuesday

Friday

Wednesday

Thursday

Fill in the blank spaces. Use the wheel to help you.

The third day of the week is _____

The day before Friday is _____

The day after Sunday is _____

The last day of the week is _____

The two days at the weekend are _____

How many months can you call out in 5 minutes? Can you get them in the right order?

Talk through the days of the week. Have a discussion to decide which is the first day. Talk through which days are school days, etc.

More words to change

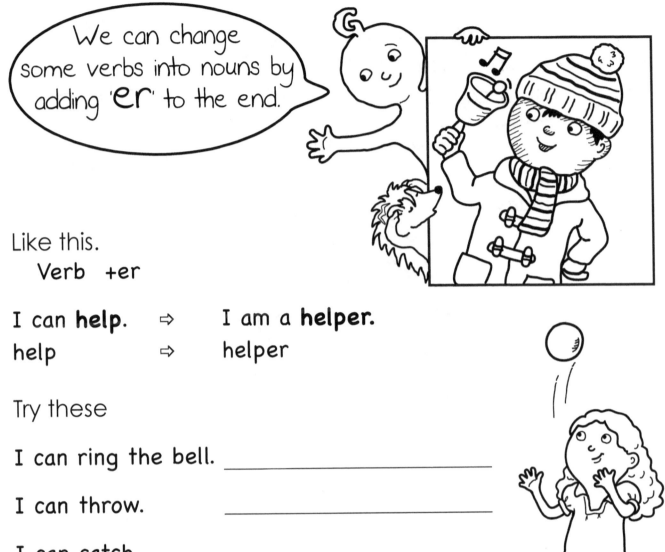

We can change some verbs into nouns by adding 'er' to the end.

Like this.

Verb +er

I can **help**. ⇨ I am a **helper**.
help ⇨ helper

Try these

I can ring the bell. _____

I can throw. _____

I can catch. _____

I can sing. _____

I can read. _____

I can walk. _____

I can jump. _____

In pairs talk about all the things you are both good at. Can you fit 'er' on to any of them?

Talk through all the text. Not all verbs morph easily into nouns! Try to find words which do. Talk about the word 'jumper' and its two meanings. Make a display bank from children's suggestions.

Brilliant Activities for Grammar and Punctuation, Year 1
© Irene Yates and Brilliant Publications

Capital letters

Capital letters are always used for:

the first letter of a sentence	the first letter of days of the week, months and special times

the first letter of a person's name; of towns, cities and countries	when talking about yourself

Underline the words that should begin with a capital letter.

house	teacher	gemma	monday
class	cup	day	diwali
london	manchester	dinosaur	christmas
holiday	friday	ryan	pencil
france	bucket	africa	miss smith

What about these sentences? Can you put them right?

i can read. _____

it is sunny today. _____

soon it will be holiday time.

_____

i will see you at christmas.

_____

Think of as many words as you can in 5 minutes that don't need to have a capital letter.

Ask children to give you lots of words that should begin with a capital letter, before they do the task sheet.

Brilliant Activities for Grammar and Punctuation, Year 1
© Irene Yates and Brilliant Publications

This page may be photocopied for use by the purchasing institution only.

39

Full stops

At the end of every sentence is a punctuation mark.

A sentence that tells you something ends with a full stop.

Put the full stops in these sentences:

The dog barked
The cat hissed
The dog jumped up
The cat spat
The dog ran away
The cat chased the dog

Copy out the text below putting in the capital letters and the full stops where they belong.

there was a fight in the garden the dog saw the cat and it barked the cat hissed and spat it frightened the dog the dog jumped out of its skin the cat was spitting and hissing the dog turned and ran with the cat chasing it i don't know who won

Talk with a friend about why we have punctuation marks. How do they help make it easier to read?

Emphasise that punctuation is there to help the reader's understanding. Make sure they understand the terms capital letter, sentence and full stop.

Question marks

A sentence that asks a question ends with a question mark (?) instead of a full stop.

Put the question marks in these sentences:

What day is it
Who are you
Where are you going
What are you doing
Why are you here
How do you do

Put the capital letters and question marks into these sentences:

what is your name where do you live do you like pizza can you stay and play have you seen the cat is it going to rain what shall we play why is the cat hiding

Here's a challenge: Get into groups of three or four. One starts by asking a question but whoever replies has to answer with another question. Then, the next person's reply also has to be a question.
How long can you keep going?

Work through the page verbally with the children tracking the text. Scribe where necessary. Reinforce the concept of question.

Exclamation marks

An exclamation mark (!) is used at the end of a sentence that shows a strong feeling. Sometimes these sentences are very short like:

Ouch!   Wow!   Well done!

Put the exclamation marks into these sentences:

Goal

Look out

What a lovely dog

Stop thief

I've won

Put the capital letters and exclamation marks into these sentences:

help there's a spider it's bigger than a mouse it's in the bath it's coming to get me i'm not scared i've turned on the tap it's running along it's really fast help help i've got it i've got it oh meet my new pet

Think of things to say to each other that need an exclamation mark.

Work through the page verbally with the children tracking the text. Reinforce the concept of strong emotion.

Brilliant Activities for Grammar and Punctuation, Year 1
© Irene Yates and Brilliant Publications

The 'me' word

There is one word that is always a capital letter. That word is 'I'.

Answer these questions about yourself using sentences starting with 'I'. Remember to make 'I' a capital letter.

1. What do you like to eat for breakfast?

_____

2. How do you get to school?

_____

3. Who do you like to sit next to at school?

_____

4. What do you like to do at break time?

_____

5. What do you do after school?

_____

6. What time do you go to bed?

_____

_____

> **Tell your partner 3 things about yourself. Start each sentence with I. Can your partner remember them all?**

Talk through the activity before the children fill in the sheet.

Un – what?

When you add 'un' to the beginning of a word it changes the meaning of that word to the opposite, like this:

pack + un = unpack
kind + un = unkind

Add 'un' to these words to change them:

do + un = _____

cover + un = _____

tie + un = _____

dress + un = _____

happy + un = _____

fair + un = _____

Make a list of more words beginning with 'un'.

_____

_____

_____

_____

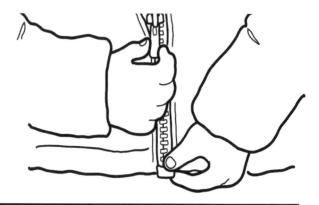

How many 'un' words can you think of in 5 minutes?

Talk about how the 'un' changes a word to make it mean its opposite. There is no need to use the term 'prefix' at this stage.

Make a story

To make a story you have to get all the sentences in the right order.

Cut and paste these sentences to make a story.

Give the story a title and write an ending sentence of your own to finish the story off. Illustrate it.

At first the birds were timid and shy.

He filled them with peanuts and hung them on the fence.

They came, had a look around, and flew away again.

Dad got some bird feeders.

All was well until a squirrel found them.

Soon they were bold enough to hang on the feeders and peck at the nuts.

Work in pairs and tell a story each, putting the sentences in the wrong order.

Read through the sentences slowly with the children tracking them. Talk about the sequence. Have the children work in pairs to cut, stick and paste. Test out new sentences verbally.

The right order

Read these sentences, then cut and paste them in the right order to make a story. Finish the story with your own sentences and illustrate it.

✂ --

It waved its trunk from side to side.

It was huge.

The elephant looked around.

In our playground!

We were in the playground one day when an elephant trundled in.

Nobody knew what to do.

We all stood still and stared.

An elephant!

Who would believe it?

Discuss with a friend how the story could end.

Read through the sentences with the children tracking the words. Talk about sequencing and verbalise different sequences to test out the story aloud. Compose the end of the story together.

Brilliant Activities for Grammar and Punctuation, Year 1
© Irene Yates and Brilliant Publications

Word banks

Word bank of nouns:

Add some more nouns

ant	day	leg	rat		
bag	end	lip	sea		
bed	farm	man	snow		
cap	fox	mum	sun		
cat	girl	net	tree		
cup	hen	pen	van		
dad	jug	pig	water		

Word bank of verbs:

Add some more verbs

add	feel	hug	run	eat	
am	find	is	sit	hop	
be	get	jump	stop	play	
bite	go	keep	tell	wish	
cry	had	look	use		
cut	has	mix	was		
do	hit	nip	were		

Word bank of adjectives:

Add some more adjectives

all	fat	little	small	dry	
bad	good	new	tidy		
best	green	old	tiny		
big	hot	red	wet		
cool	kind	shy	white		

Punctuation marks

I know these punctuation marks and these are my examples:

Capital letters:

Full stops:

Exclamation marks:

Question marks:

Brilliant Activities for Grammar and Punctuation, Year 1
© Irene Yates and Brilliant Publications

Assessment checklist

Name:		Term	
	1	2	3
Can understand and use the following terminology:			
Letter			
Capital letter			
Singular			
Plural			
Sentence			
Punctuation			
Full stop			
Question mark			
Exclamation mark			
Understands and is able to:			
Name the letters of the alphabet in order			
Put words into alphabetical order, using 1st letter			
Write a proper sentence with correct punctuation			
Use 'and' to combine sentences to make a longer sentence			
Make a singular noun plural by adding 's'			
Make a singular noun starting with s, x, or ch plural by adding 'es'			
Understand that nouns are used to name things			
Understand that verbs are doing or being words			
Understand that adjectives are words that describe nouns			
Understand that when we add beginnings, such as 'un', or endings, such as 'er', to words (prefixes and suffixes), we change their meaning			
Use capital letters for people's names			
Use a capital for the pronoun 'I'			
Use capital letters for other proper nouns such as days of the week, names of places, etc			
Use capital letters, full stops, question marks and exclamation marks to punctuate sentences			
Sequence sentences to form short narratives			

Answers

Alphabetical order (pg 8)
Children to write out their names in alphabetical order.

How much do you know? (pg 9)
Capital letters
Small letters
the letter third from the end is x,
7 letters before H
10 letters after P
6 letters between J and Q.
Letters before and after children's names.

Jumbled letters (pg 10)
FGH, BCDE, PQRS, efg, tuv, opqr, wxyz, lmno.

Is it a sentence? (pg 12)
1. no, 2. no, 3. yes, 4. no, 5. yes, 6. yes, 7. no, 8. no, 9. no.

Making sentences (pg 15)
The girl baked a cake/ went swimming.
The dog barked at the cat.
A duck quacked.
Dad went swimming/ baked a cake.
Robins can fly.
A camel has humps.
The snail left a trail.

Add an ending (pg 16)
I can climb this mountain.
We wear boots for climbing.
Mountains are high.
A clock tells us the time.

And, and, and … (pg 17)
I went to the park and I played ball with a friend.
I saw a girl on a skateboard and she fell off.
I went to the cafe and I bought a bottle of water.
There were lots of geese and they chased me.
It started to rain and I went home.

Nouns are names (pg 19)
Dog, ears, tail, eyes, nose, collar, paws, legs, fur.

What can you see? (pg 20)
clouds, trees, a lake, a sailboat, reeds, a girl, a kite, an ice-cream van, some flowers, some children, a slide, some swings, a lady, a balloon, an ice lolly, an ice-cream, a boy, some dogs.

Noun puzzle (pg 21)
1. elephant, 2. star, 3. egg, 4. buggy, 5 car. 6. monkey.

Noun word puzzle (pg 22)

b	o	o	k	s	b
f	r	o	g	i	a
d	u	c	k	n	b
n	s	e	o	g	y
m	o	o	n	w	z

… a bike

One or more than one? (pg 23)
two cats, two boats, three horses, four elephants, two dinosaurs, three trees, three boys, four girls.

Different endings (pg 24)
buses, glasses, dresses, kisses, classes, foxes, boxes, witches, pitches, churches.

Make a sentence (pg 26)
I love playing football.
My friend likes ice-cream.
Our dog barks at people.
My teacher makes us laugh.
We are going on a trip.
Birds have feathers.
Cats have whiskers.
My dad likes the weekend.
On Mondays we always have circle time.
The boys want to play.

Joining sentences (pg 27)
Bees buzz and they collect pollen.
Birds have feathers and they build nests.
Snakes are long and they lay eggs.
Elephants are huge and they have tusks.
Cats have fur and they meow.
Lions are big cats and they roar.
Rabbits have big ears and they twitch their noses.

Brilliant Activities for Grammar and Punctuation, Year 1
© Irene Yates and Brilliant Publications

Which are? (pg 29)

a shady tree, a good story, a yellow bird, a green frog, a happy girl, a laughing boy.

Green, yellow, blue, soft, round, strong.

Cut and stick (pg 30)

small mouse, cold ice lolly, fast car, long tail, sharp knife, deep water, open door, soft pillow, ripe banana, dry washing, cheeky monkey.

What do you think? (pg 31)

1. weather, 2. doughnut, 3. book, 4. shoe, 5. frog, 6.rabbit.

What's a verb? (pg 32)

I can hop, I can jump, I can dance, I can sit, I can run, I can see, I can walk, I can mix.

Changing the words (pg 33)

eat/eating, jump/jumping, fall/falling, sail/sailing, talk/talking, read/reading, drink/drinking, work/working, fish/fishing, fly/flying.

Verbs and nouns together (pg 34)

A duck quacks. A dog barks. A cat purrs. A bird flies. The Sun shines. A boat sails. A fish swims. The fish is swimming. The clock is ticking. The boat is sailing.

Make a proper sentence (pg 35)

1. bounced, 2. rang, 3. peeled, 4. ate, 5. paddled, 6. dance, 7. closed.

Days of the week (pg 37)

Wednesday, Thursday, Monday, Sunday, Saturday and Sunday.

Note: If you agree as a class to start with a different day, your answers will be different.

More words to change (pg 38)

ringer, thrower, catcher, singer, reader, walker, jumper.

Capital letters (pg 39)

Gemma, Monday, Diwali, London, Manchester, Christmas, Friday, Ryan, France, Africa, Miss Smith.

I can read. It is sunny today. Soon it will be holiday time. I will see you at Christmas.

Full stops (pg 40)

The dog barked. The cat hissed. The dog jumped. The cat spat. The dog ran away. The cat chased the dog.

There was a fight in the garden. The dog saw the cat and it barked. The cat hissed and spat.

It frightened the dog. The dog jumped out of its skin. The cat was spitting and hissing. The dog turned and ran with the cat chasing it. I don't know who won.

Question marks (pg 41)

What day is it? Who are you? Where are you going? What are you doing? Why are you here? How do you do?

What is your name? Where do you live? Do you like pizza? Can you stay and play? Have you seen the cat? Is it going to rain? What shall we play? Why is the cat hiding?

Exclamation marks (pg 42)

Goal! Look out! What a lovely dog! Stop thief! I've won!

Help! There's a spider. It's bigger than a mouse! It's in the bath. It's coming to get me! I'm not scared. I've turned on the tap. It's running along. It's really fast. Help! Help! I've got it! I've got it! Oh meet my new pet!

Un – what? (pg 44)

undo, uncover, untie, undress, unhappy, unfair.

Make a story (pg 45)

Dad got some bird feeders. He filled them with peanuts and hung them on the fence. At first the birds were timid and shy. They came, had a look around, and flew away again. Soon they were bold enough to hang on the feeders and peck at the nuts. All was well until a squirrel found them.

The right order (pg 46)

We were in the playground one day when an elephant trundled in. It was huge. The elephant looked around. It waved its trunk from side to side. Nobody knew what to do. We all stood still and stared. Who would believe it? An elephant! In our playground!

(Accept other sensible combinations.)

CPSIA information can be obtained
at www.ICGtesting.com
Printed in the USA
LVHW100717190219
607997LV00011B/447/P